Dear Parent:
Your child's love of reading starts here!

Every child learns to ~~read at~~ his or her own speed.
You can help your yo~~ung reader improve and beco~~me more confident
by encouraging his o~~r her own interests and skills~~. You can also guide
your child's spiritual ~~growth by reading stories with b~~iblical values
and Bible stories, lik~~e this one published by Zon~~derkidz. From
books your child rec~~eives as gifts to the books he or she~~ reads alone,
there are I Can Rea~~d books for every stage of reading:~~

JONES
Daniel, God's faithful
follower

SHARED READING
Basic language, word repetition, and whimsical
illustrations, ideal for sharing with your emergent reader.

BEGINNING READING
Short sentences, familiar words, and simple concepts for
children eager to read on their own.

READING WITH HELP
Engaging stories, longer sentences, and language play
for developing readers.

READING ALONE
Complex plots, challenging vocabulary, and high-interest
topics for the independent reader.

ADVANCED READING
Short paragraphs, chapters, and exciting themes for the
perfect bridge to chapter books.

I Can Read! books have introduced children to the joy of reading since
1957. Featuring award-winning authors and illustrators and a fabulous
cast of beloved characters, I Can Read! books set the standard for
beginning readers.

A lifetime of discovery begins with the magical words "I Can Read!"

Visit www.icanread.com for information on enriching your child's reading experience.
Visit www.zonderkidz.com for more Zonderkidz I Can Read! titles.

APR   2011

Lord, I call out to you.
Come quickly to help me.
—Psalm 141:1

ZONDERKIDZ

Daniel, God's Faithful Follower
Copyright © 2010 by Zondervan
Illustrations © 2010 by Dennis G. Jones

Requests for information should be addressed to:

Zondervan, *Grand Rapids, Michigan* 49530

Library of Congress Cataloging-in-Publication Data

Jones, Dennis, 1956-
    Daniel, God's faithful follower / pictures by Dennis Jones.
       p. cm. — (I can read!) (Dennis Jones series)
    ISBN 978-0-310-71834-5 (softcover)
    1. Daniel (Biblical figure)—Juvenile literature. I. Title.
    BS580.D2J66 2010
    224'.509505—dc22   2009047262

Published in association with the literary agency of Alive Communications, Inc., 7680 God-
dard Street #200, Colorado Springs, CO 80920. www.alivecommunications.com

Zonderkidz is a trademark of Zondervan.

Editor: Mary Hassinger
Art direction and design: Sarah Molegraaf

Printed in China

---

10 11 12 13 14 /SCC/ 5 4 3 2 1

DANIEL
God's Faithful Follower

pictures by Dennis G. Jones

Long ago, there was a good man named Daniel.

He helped the king rule the land.

The king loved Daniel very much.

Some of the king's other helpers
were jealous of Daniel.
So they had a plan to get
him in trouble!

Daniel loved God very much.

He prayed to him three times a day.

The king's other helpers did not
like that and made up a new law.
"People can only pray to
the king … or else!"

Daniel heard about the law.

He went home to pray.

He wanted to talk to God
about the new law.

The men were watching to see
what Daniel would do.

Would Daniel break the new law?

Daniel prayed, "Dear God!
I love you. I do not like to
disobey rules, but I will never
stop praying to you!"

The men watched Daniel pray.

They were very happy to see

Daniel praying to his God.

He was breaking the new law!

"Daniel, you are not following
the new law—
Do not pray to anyone but the king!"
said the men.
"I will never stop praying to God,"
said Daniel.

So the men took Daniel to see the king.

They said, "King, remember
your new law?

We saw Daniel pray to his God!

He broke the law!"

The king was very sad.

He thought about how

to rescue his friend Daniel.

But he did not have a plan.

"You must follow the rules,"
the men told the king.
And so the king took Daniel
to the lion's den.

The sad king said good-bye to
his friend Daniel.

Daniel said good-bye to the king.

The men were happy!

They had finally gotten the good man

Daniel in trouble!

Daniel was going to be thrown

into the lion's den.

Daniel was thrown into the lion's den.

The men smiled as they watched

him fall down, down, down

into the den.

Daniel thought to himself,

"I am in trouble!"

Daniel looked at the hungry lions.

The hungry lions looked at Daniel.

He knew what to do!

Daniel knew he needed to pray

to God for help,

just like he did every day!

Daniel knelt on the ground.

He started praying to God

for protection.

God heard Daniel's prayers
loud and clear!
An angel appeared and shut
the lions' mouths.

All night long, Daniel prayed to God.
All night long, God's angel
kept the lions away from Daniel.
Daniel talked to God
and thanked him
for the angel's help.

27

In the morning, the king ran

to the lion's den.

"Daniel!" the king shouted.

"How are you, my friend?"

Daniel smiled at the king.

"I am safe! God sent an angel.

He kept the lions away all night long."

The king smiled too.

"Get Daniel out of that lion's den,"

the king said.

The king was happy that
God had kept Daniel safe.
He told all of his people about
Daniel's God.

The king said,

"God is a great God!"

The king had the

other helpers arrested.

That night, Daniel prayed,

"Thank you, God. You ARE great!"